UNDERSTANDING VIRUSES

STAYING SAFE FROM VIRUSES

AV2
www.av2books.com

Heather C. Hudak

Step 1
Go to **www.av2books.com**

Step 2
Enter this unique code

PCOLHVCGW

Step 3
Explore your interactive eBook!

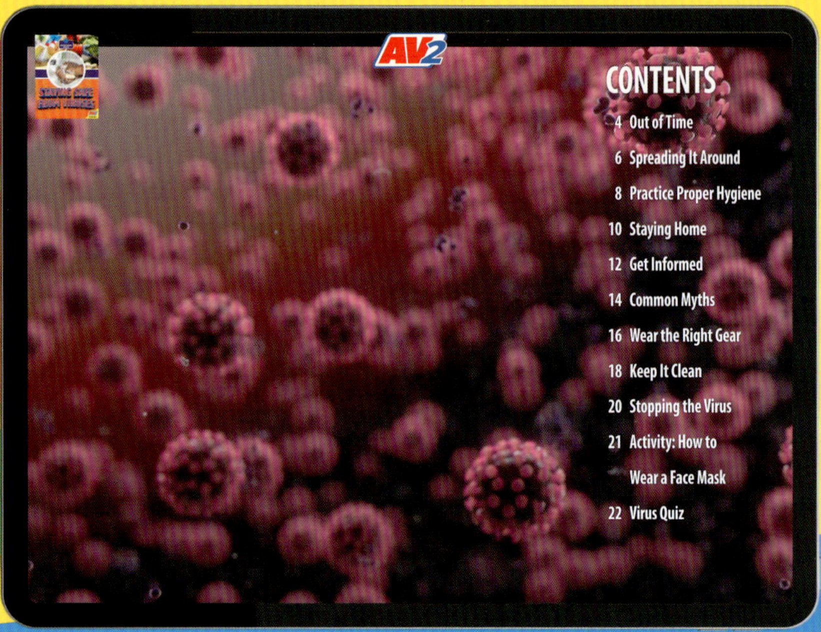

AV2 is optimized for use on any device

Your interactive eBook comes with...

Contents
Browse a live contents page to easily navigate through resources

Audio
Listen to sections of the book read aloud

Videos
Watch informative video clips

Weblinks
Gain additional information for research

Try This!
Complete activities and hands-on experiments

Key Words
Study vocabulary, and complete a matching word activity

Quizzes
Test your knowledge

Slideshows
View images and captions

... and much, much more!

STAYING SAFE FROM VIRUSES

CONTENTS

Out of Time

In late 2019, a new virus made hundreds of people sick in Wuhan, China. Scientists called the virus COVID-19. Within months, it had spread to people all over the world. Countries closed their borders. They did not want the virus to get in or out. People were told to stay home to stop the virus's spread. By spring 2020, millions of people were sick. Many had died.

Health workers put their own lives at risk to save others. However, they began to run out of supplies. They did not have the proper gear to protect themselves from the virus. There were not enough gowns, masks, or gloves. Some health workers were given one mask to use for as long as they could. They cleaned their masks between patients. However, they feared it was not enough. They did not want to infect people who were not yet ill. Companies were asked to make more supplies, but it would take time. People were asked to donate any masks or gloves that they could spare.

People living in Wuhan were forbidden to leave their city for 76 days during the city's COVID-19 outbreak.

FAST FACT

U.S. health workers would need more than 3.5 billion masks for a severe outbreak that lasted one year. They only had about 1 percent of that number available at the beginning of the COVID-19 pandemic.

Spreading It Around

People come in contact with millions of germs each day. Some of these germs are viruses. Viruses are tiny **parasites**. They cause many different diseases. Some, such as the flu, are common. They spread quickly. Others, such as Ebola, are rare. They do not spread easily.

A sneeze can spread infected droplets as far as 27 feet (8.2 meters) away.

It is important to reduce the risk of coming into contact with a virus, no matter how it spreads.

Small droplets come out of the nose and mouth when a person coughs or sneezes. Other people might breathe in these droplets. Droplets can also land on objects. The virus may spread if a person touches the **infected** object and then touches his or her eyes, nose, mouth, or any breaks in the skin. Many viruses, such as COVID-19 and the common cold, spread through droplets.

Other Ways Viruses Spread

Some viruses can spread through **bodily fluids.** Others spread through **contaminated** water. Viruses can also be spread by infected animals. People can come into contact with or be bitten by these animals.

Practice Proper Hygiene

Some viruses can live on a person's body or clothes for a while. It is important for people to keep clean in order to help remove these germs.

People touch their eyes, nose, and mouth all the time. By washing their hands, they can remove harmful germs that could infect them when this happens. Proper handwashing requires soap and water. It takes about 20 seconds.

Bathing is another important part of **hygiene**. People need to scrub their entire body. People also need to keep their mouths clean. Germs can build up in the mouth. Brushing the teeth for two minutes twice a day helps break these germs down. Germs often build up under a person's nails, too. Trimming the nails can help keep them clean.

Tools used to maintain personal hygiene, such as nail clippers, shower sponges, or towels, should not be shared with other people.

Freshwater Availability

About 2 billion people live in areas where fresh water for drinking and bathing is scarce. This map shows the parts of the world that are most affected by water scarcity.

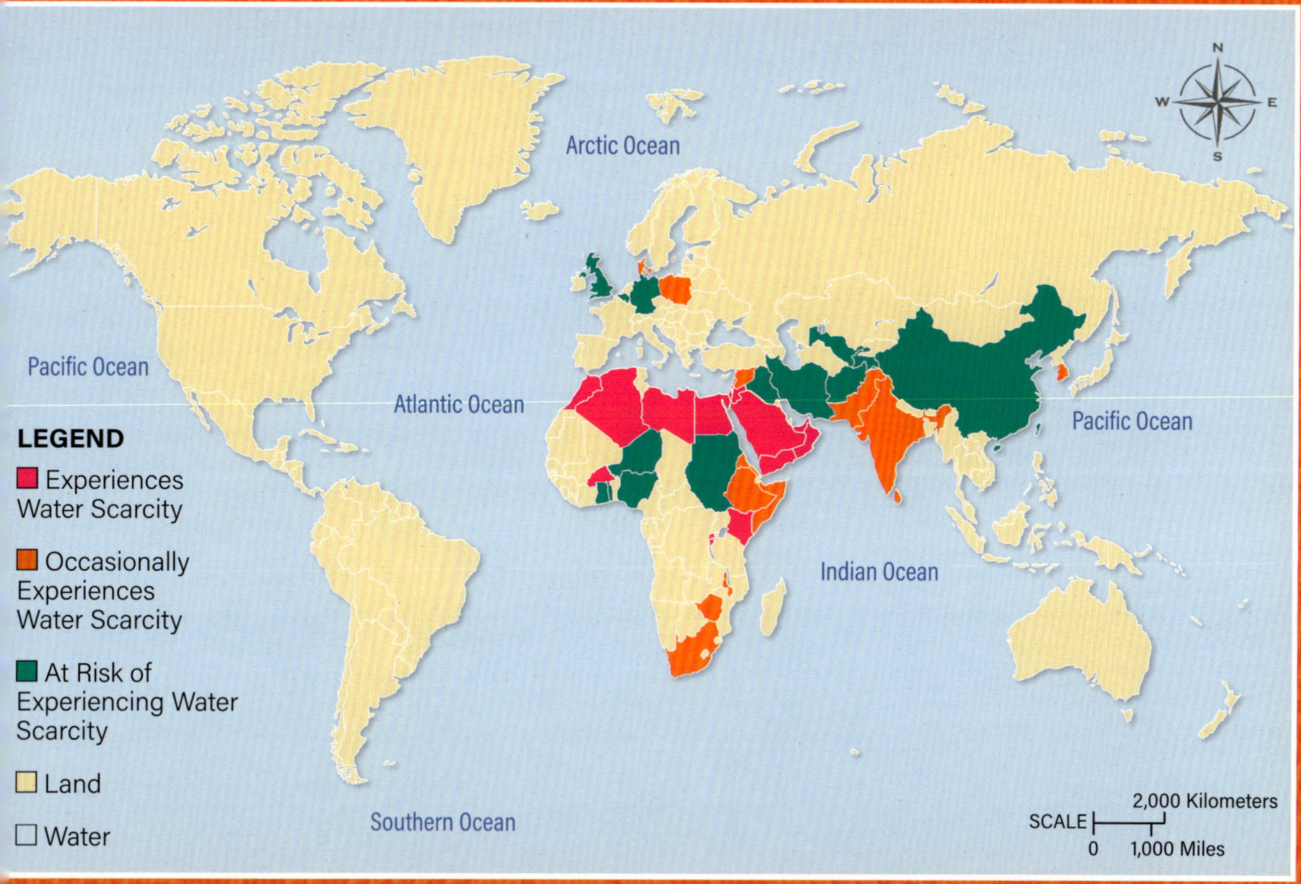

Scientists estimate that, by 2030, up to 700 million people might have to leave their homes due to water scarcity.

Staying Home

People who feel unwell should try to avoid others. This helps stop the spread of a virus. The more contact people have with an infected person, the faster a virus can spread. Staying home helps protect others from getting sick.

Symptoms can last longer or get worse when people do not take time to rest. Most times, people do not need to see a doctor if they have a virus. People can recognize the symptoms on their own. They only need to go to the doctor if a virus's symptoms last more than a few days or are worse than normal.

Eating a balanced diet and getting enough sleep can help people who feel unwell get better faster.

Greeting others with a wave instead of a handshake or hug helps limit the spread of germs between people.

Keep Your Distance

Social distancing means avoiding direct contact with other people. It is used to slow the spread of a disease. It involves changing day-to-day activities to limit direct interactions with others. This means staying away from crowded places such as malls, parks, and concerts. It also means people should try to work and study from home if they can. Experts recommend keeping a distance of at least 6 feet (1.8 m) from other people when practicing social distancing.

Get Informed

Sometimes there is an outbreak of a virus. An outbreak happens when many people unexpectedly get sick at the same time. It is important to learn the facts and stay up to date about outbreaks. There is a lot of information about diseases on the internet and news. Not all of it is true. It is always a good idea to get the facts from health experts.

The World Health Organization (WHO) is part of the **United Nations**. WHO helps keep people around the world healthy. It provides details about how to stay safe in an outbreak. The Centers for Disease Control and Prevention (CDC) is part of the U.S. government. It gives guidance on how people in the United States can protect against diseases. Local experts also give out information about their communities. People should be sure to follow their doctor's orders if they are sick. This means taking medications as **prescribed**.

People can visit official websites of institutions such as the WHO and CDC to have the most up-to-date information about outbreaks of a disease.

Family doctors can help people in a community stay informed about outbreaks.

Flattening the Curve

There may not be enough doctors or supplies to help everyone in an outbreak. If this happens, authorities may recommend measures to help lower the number of people who get sick each day. When a virus spreads at a slower pace, doctors have a better chance to help everyone. This is called flattening the curve.

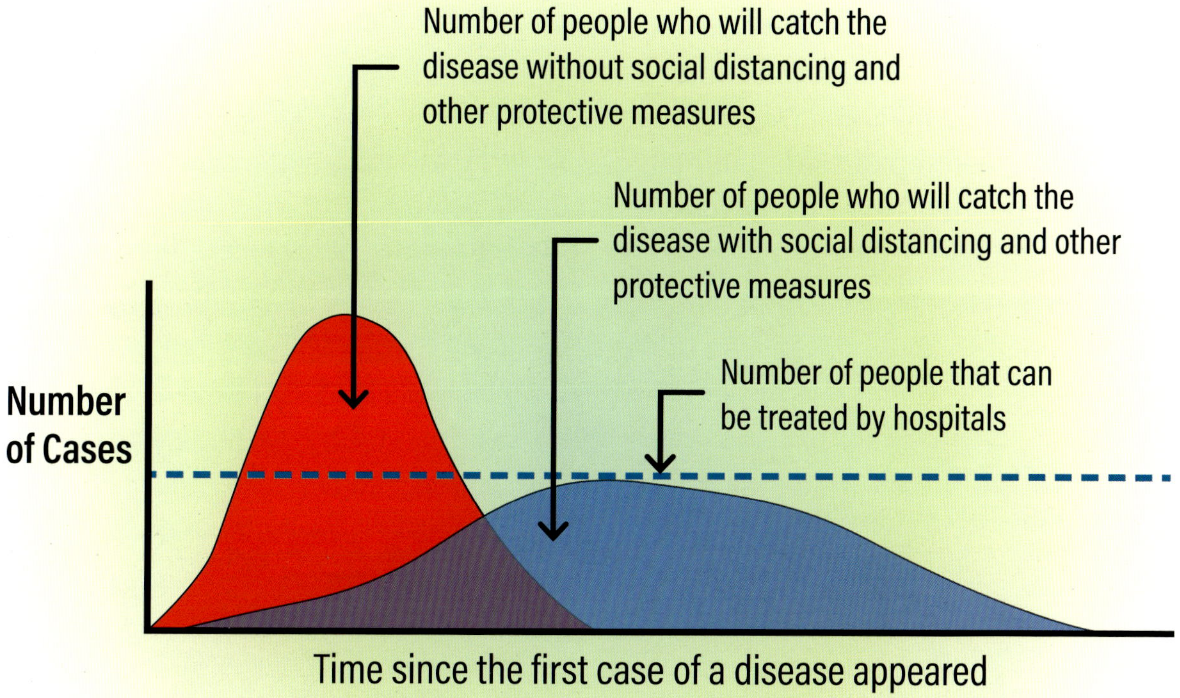

Common Myths

There are many myths about viruses. People should learn the facts so they can then make good choices about how to protect themselves.

Antibiotics Kill Viruses

Antibiotics are a type of medication. They help stop infections caused by **bacteria**. Antibiotics do not help stop infections caused by viruses. Taking antibiotics when they are not needed lowers the chance of them working when they are needed.

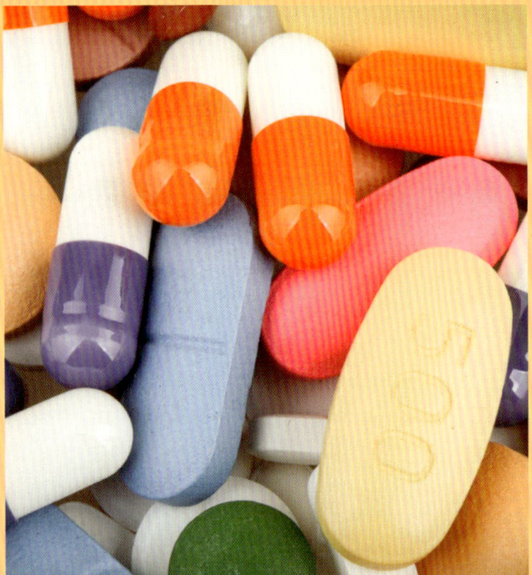

Dressing Warm in Winter Protects against Viruses

Some viruses are more common in winter. Many people think this is because of the cold. They dress warmer than needed. People tend to stay inside together when the weather is cold. This is what makes it more likely for them to catch a virus from another person during the cold months.

Exercise Helps Cure Viruses

Exercise can help keep people from getting sick in the first place. However, people should not exercise if they have symptoms of a virus. It can make them feel worse if they have a cough, upset stomach, or aches and pains.

Flu Is a Mild Disease

Most people with the flu feel sick only for a few days, but the flu can be deadly. This is why it is important to get a flu shot every year.

Over-the-Counter Medications Can Cure Diseases

Over-the-counter medications are popular products during flu and cold season. People who use them often believe they can cure these viruses. In fact, these medications only help with the symptoms but cannot cure the diseases.

Hold Your Breath for 10 Seconds to Find Out if You Have a Disease

Some believe that people who cannot hold their breath for 10 seconds could be sick with a disease of the lungs. However, this might not be true. Only a **medical** expert can **diagnose** a disease.

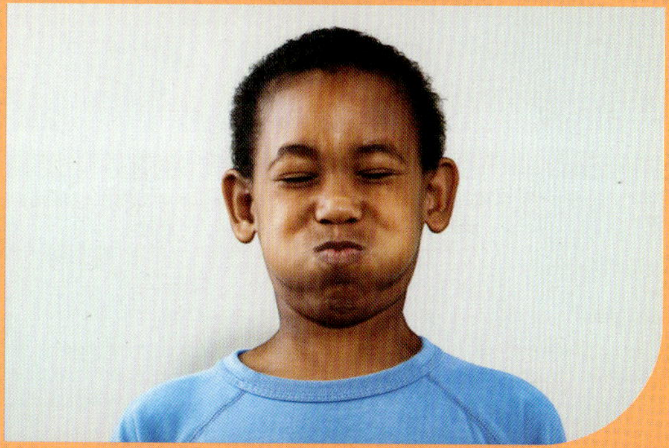

Wear the Right Gear

Face masks help catch droplets that could spread a virus when a person coughs or sneezes. People can wear face masks if they leave the house or go near others. Health workers and caregivers wear medical face masks when helping sick people who might infect them with a virus. They may also wear disposable gowns, coveralls, and gloves to keep from coming into contact with bodily fluids that might contain the virus.

People who have trouble breathing should not wear face masks.

People can hang nets around their beds to keep insects away while they sleep.

Some viruses, such as Zika virus and the West Nile virus, spread through insect bites. It is important to wear the proper gear in places where insects are known to carry these viruses. People should wear long-sleeved shirts and long pants to cover as much skin as they can. They can also use insect repellent to help keep these insects from biting.

FAST FACT

There are about 3,000 kinds of mosquitoes around the world. Three types, *Anopheles*, *Aedes*, and *Culex* mosquitoes, are the ones known to spread the most diseases.

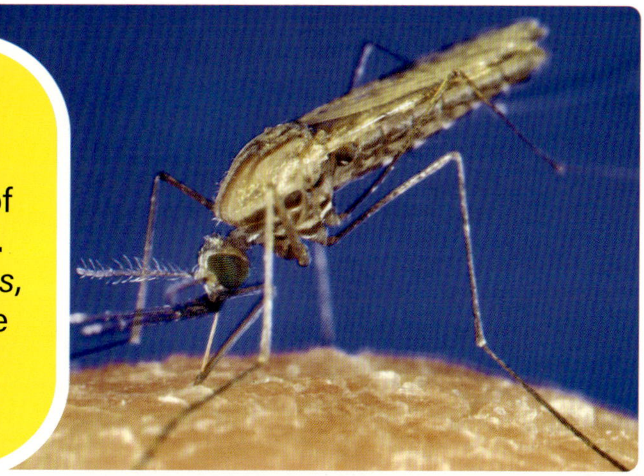

Keep It Clean

Viruses can be found anywhere. They are found on floors and counters. They can be inside the shower and on toys. They can even be on food. Proper hygiene helps protect against viruses and other kinds of germs. Surfaces should be cleaned often using **detergents**. **Disinfectants** contain chemicals that help kill viruses. For instance, bleach or alcohol mixed with water are good to use on hard surfaces.

Germs can spread through contaminated foods. The best way to make sure food does not contain germs is to cook it. Fresh fruit and vegetables need to be washed well before they are cut or eaten in order to remove any germs.

Tap water and well water are not safe to drink in some parts of the world. **Filters** cannot remove viruses from water. Viruses are so small that they flow right through the filter. If there is no source of clean water, people need to boil water before drinking it. They can also drink bottled water instead.

Keeping water at its boiling point for at least 1 minute is one of the most effective ways to make it safe from waterborne viruses.

The Dirtiest Things in the Home

Many objects people use everyday are germ-infested. Here is a list of dirty items we use in our daily lives. Remember to clean these frequently.

Computer Keyboards: People use keyboards every day for study or work. In many cases, people share them with others, allowing germs to circulate more.

Kitchen Sponges: Food residue and moisture make kitchen sponges the perfect home for germs. These sponges should be replaced at least once a week.

Bathroom Sink: When people wash their hands, germs are transferred to the bathroom sink's surface. To avoid the spread of germs, the sink should be sanitized frequently.

Reusable Water Bottle: These items can often spread germs. People carry them around, touch them with unclean hands, and do not wash them frequently enough.

Shoes: Shoe soles are used everywhere but are rarely cleaned. They can carry very dangerous germs. People should not wear dirty shoes around the house.

Stopping the Virus

Viruses attack a person's cells. Then, they make copies of themselves and spread throughout the body. White blood cells fight back against the virus. It can take time for the body to build up enough white blood cells to make a difference. If a person gets the same virus again, the white blood cells remember it. The body has some **immunity** for the virus.

Vaccines help boost a person's immunity, too. They work by giving a person a small, safe amount of a virus. The body can then get used to the virus and learn how to fight it. Vaccines save millions of lives each year.

Not all viruses have a vaccine. Scientists work to make new ones all the time. Vaccines can take years to make.

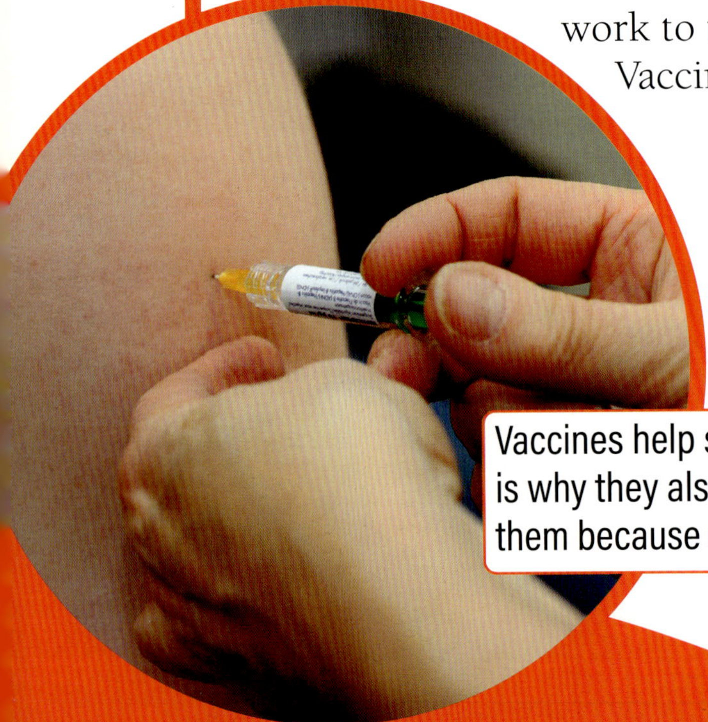

Vaccines help stop the spread of a virus. This is why they also help people who cannot get them because of medical conditions.

ACTIVITY

How to Wear a Face Mask

Face masks only protect people if they are worn properly.

Always follow these steps when wearing a face mask.

1. Wash your hands before touching the mask.
2. Place the straps around the back of your head.
3. Make sure the mask covers your mouth and nose. There should not be any gaps between your face and the mask.
4. Do not touch the front of the mask when you have it on or when you remove it.
5. Replace the mask when it becomes wet or dirty.
6. Do not wear single-use masks more than once.
7. Thoroughly wash reusable masks.

- Why should these steps be followed when wearing a face mask?
- Who is protected by wearing a mask?
- What kinds of face masks should people wear?

Research online and at the library to answer these questions.

VIRUS QUIZ

1
What is a virus?

2
What does the CDC do?

3
How long should proper handwashing last?

4
How does a virus spread?

5
What is social distancing?

6
How far can a sneeze spread infected droplets?

7
How can people protect against insect bites?

8
Which types of mosquitoes are more likely to spread diseases?

ANSWERS

1. A tiny parasite 2. It gives people in the United States guidance on how to protect against viruses 3. 20 seconds 4. Contact with infected people, animals, food, water, objects, or bodily fluids 5. Avoiding contact with others 6. Up to 27 feet (8.2 m) 7. By wearing long sleeves and pants, using insect repellent, hanging a net over their beds 8. *Anopheles*, *Aedes*, and *Culex* mosquitoes

Key Words

bacteria: tiny organisms, each made of one cell
bodily fluids: fluids that come from the body, such as blood or saliva
contaminated: made impure or harmful
detergents: cleaning agents that remove dirt and grime
diagnose: recognize a disease through a medical examination
disinfectants: chemicals that destroy harmful germs
filters: devices with small openings that are used to remove unwanted materials
hygiene: steps a person takes to stay clean and healthy
immunity: the ability to ward off infections
infected: came in contact with a virus that then entered the body
medical: related to the practice of medicine
parasites: organisms that live on or inside other organisms, called hosts
prescribed: treatment based on a doctor's orders
symptoms: body changes that are consequences of a disease
United Nations: an organization that helps maintain world peace and gets countries to work together on common issues

Index

Published by AV2
14 Penn Plaza, 9th Floor
New York, NY 10122
Website: www.av2books.com

Library of Congress Control Number: 2020940984

ISBN 978-1-7911-3262-0 (hardcover)
ISBN 978-1-7911-3263-7 (softcover)
ISBN 978-1-7911-3264-4 (multi-user eBook)
ISBN 978-1-7911-3265-1 (single-user eBook)

Printed in Guangzhou, China
1 2 3 4 5 6 7 8 9 0 24 23 22 21 20

072020
101119

Project Coordinator: Sara Cucini
Designer: Terry Paulhus

Every reasonable effort has been made to trace ownership and to obtain permission to reprint copyright material. The publisher would be pleased to have any errors or omissions brought to their attention so that they may be corrected in subsequent printings.

AV2 acknowledges Getty Images, iStock, and Shutterstock as its primary image suppliers for this title.